I0440925

Hummingbird Stories
WeeBean & William

A story about
a little boy and his friend,
a baby hummingbird.

by
Sandy Lizotte

The hummingbirds had a long
flight from the south,
and returned to their favorite
nesting place.
The air was alive with
hummingbirds,
and they darted back and forth
like tiny helicopters.

*Did you know? Hummingbirds are only found
in North and South America.*

A beautiful hummingbird
named Cheryl
was looking
for a mate.

*Did you know? There are more than 320
known hummingbird species.*

She found a brilliant
male to be the father
of her babies.

Did you know? The male hummingbird is
more colorful than the female, when fully mature.

Cheryl built her nest
in the backyard
of a little boy
named William.

*Did you know? Hummingbirds build their nests
from spider webs, thin grass, cotton, feathers,
bark, moss, and lichens.*

One day seven year old
William was playing in
his backyard when he
noticed a hummingbird
sitting on a nest.

*Did you know? North American hummingbird
nests are about the size of a golf ball.*

Cheryl only laid one egg,
and William patiently waited
everyday to see the
new born baby hatch.

*Did you know? Hummingbirds usually
lay two eggs. The eggs will normally
hatch in 14 - 18 days.*

William was amazed to see
how tiny the baby
hummingbird really was.
He named the baby WeeBean,
because he compared it to
the size of a tiny black bean.

*Did you know? Hummingbirds are born
without feathers and their eyes are not open.*

William liked to whistle
when he approached
the nest.
One day WeeBean
whistled back.

Did you know? Hummingbirds communicate
through calls or songs, such as chirping
clucking, chattering, peeps, or a whistle.

Whistling became a
great game between
William and his new
best friend WeeBean.

Did you know? Throughout history
there have been many stories and beliefs
about these unique little birds.

William went on a
20-day trip.
He thought about WeeBean
every night, and wanted to see
his best friend again.

*Did you know? A baby hummingbird will leave
the nest when it is approximately 23 days old.*

Mother hummingbird Cheryl
continued to feed her baby.
WeeBean was growing
fast and strong.

*Did you know? The mother hummingbird feeds
her babies a mixture of flower nectar,
small insects, and sugar water.*

WeeBean has now left the nest, and whistled for his friend William. But he could not find him.

Did you know? A baby hummingbird will return to the nest to sleep at night.

When William returned,
he found the nest was empty.
He hung a feeder and prayed
for WeeBean to come back.

*Did you know? To make hummingbird feeder solution use
one part white pure cane sugar to four parts water.
Do not use red food coloring. A stronger concentration
can be used when first attracting the birds.*

Two days later WeeBean
saw William playing.
WeeBean started to whistle.
William was so happy
to be reunited with
his best friend.

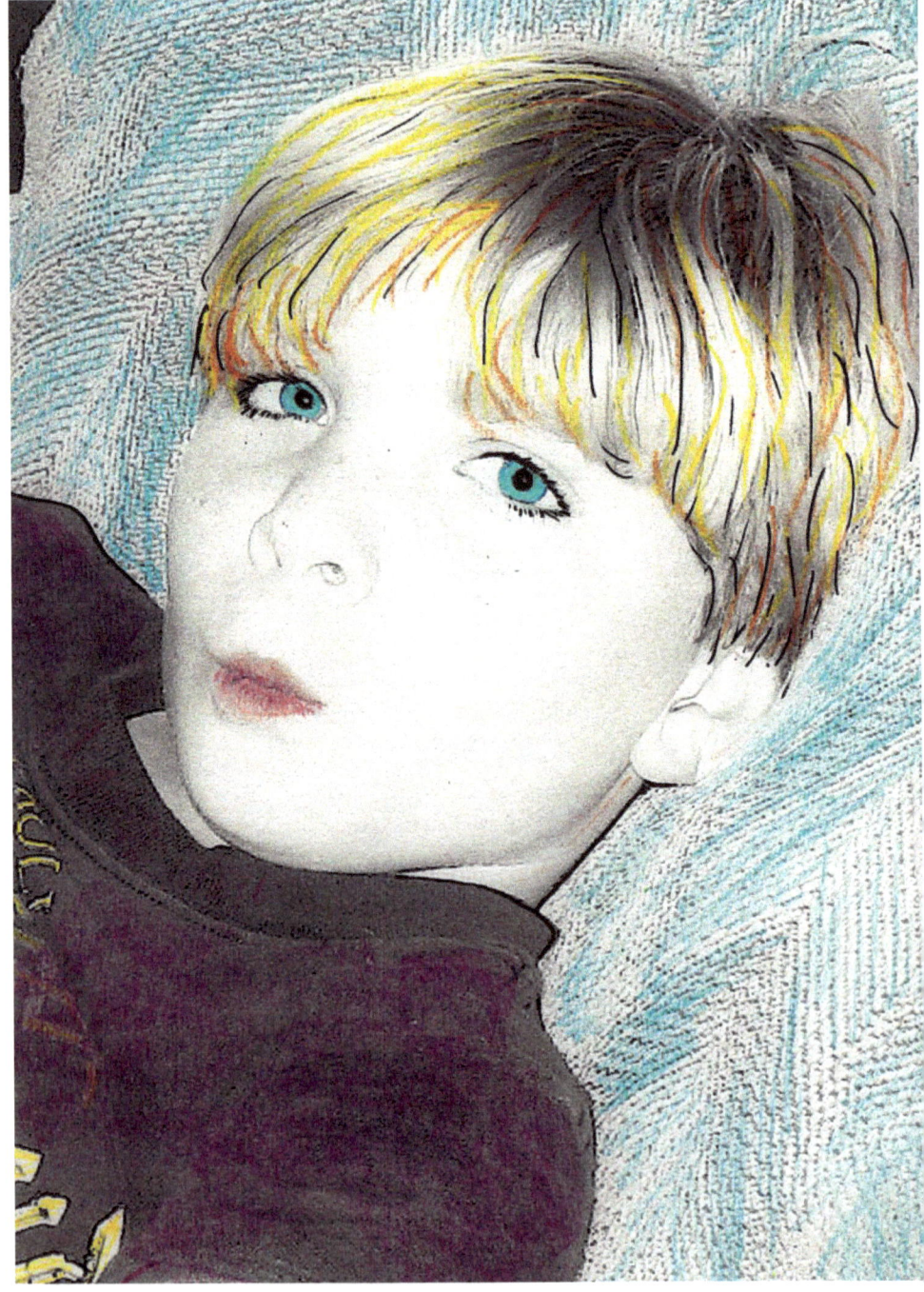

William thanked WeeBean
for becoming such a
special friend
and part of his life.
And to this day,
WeeBean whistles
and William whistles back.

Did you know? A hummingbird's average
lifespan is 3 to 5 years, and can
live for more than 10 years.

Sandy ☺

"Life is Good"

Artwork and Story
by
Sandy Lizotte

www.HummingbirdStories.com

Thank You

William Lang
Cheryl McMichael
Don DesJardin
Reni Seidman
Fritz Budworth
Mike Biallas
Jim & Inara Biallas
And all of my
supporting Friends!

www.ingramcontent.com/pod-product-compliance
Lightning Source LLC
Chambersburg PA
CBHW040317010626
45792CB00023B/707

* 9 7 8 1 4 4 8 6 5 1 8 5 6 *